Breathe...

An Anticipatory Grief Journal

Dawn Stilwell

Breathe...

An Anticipatory Grief Journal

The Publishing Shop

This Book Belongs to

_____

A Message from Dawn

My sister Jennifer passed away in November of 2021, by her choice to avail herself of a medically assisted suicide. When she switched from curative treatments for her cancer, to palliative care, it hit me quite hard that she was going to die much sooner than our family had anticipated. That is when I began to experience anticipatory grief and anxiety.

Losing a loved one is never easy. In my own experience, I think that the anticipatory grief was worse than the grief that arrived after Jennifer's death. Working with mental health advocate, Debb Pitel, on the No One Stands Alone initiative, (www.noonestandsalone.ca), I was made aware that grief counseling was available through my local hospice. As I wanted some kind of relief from the overwhelming thoughts and emotions, I made an appointment and soon after, was able to see a counselor there.

I learned a lot through those appointments. Tips on self-soothing, learning that it was ok to honor my own feelings, and being told that what I was feeling was normal for this type of situation. Having someone to talk to about what I was going through helped me a lot.

One of the things recommended to me by the counselor was to begin keeping a grief journal. If you take the time to put your thoughts and emotions and write them down, they are less likely to be intrusive, bouncing around your mind and potentially keeping you up at night. I created this grief journal, with prompts, for others who may find themselves experiencing anticipatory grief ahead of the foreknown death of a friend or loved one. I don't expect you to write daily, although you could, and I've included some journal prompts to help you along in case you don't know where to start.

It is my hope that during this tumultuous emotional time, this book will help you ground yourself and be present with all you are feeling.

I know it's hard, and you wouldn't have chosen this path willingly. It seems cliche to say you'll get through it, but you will get through it.

Breathe. Take one moment at a time. And remember, your best is enough.

Dawn

The
Grief Journal

Part One:
Identifying Feelings
& Needs

Whose foreseeable death is causing your anticipatory grief?
Write about them and their journey.

_____
_____
_____
_____
_____
_____
_____
_____
_____
_____
_____
_____
_____
_____
_____
_____
_____
_____
_____
_____
_____
_____
_____

How is this grief affecting your everyday life?

_____

_____

_____

_____

_____

_____

_____

_____

_____

_____

_____

_____

_____

_____

_____

_____

_____

_____

_____

_____

_____

_____

What is your greatest fear concerning this situation?

My support system includes:

_____

_____

_____

_____

_____

_____

_____

_____

_____

_____

_____

_____

_____

_____

_____

_____

_____

_____

_____

_____

_____

_____

_____

What is something you think you need to share with your loved one who is dying?

_____
_____
_____
_____
_____
_____
_____
_____
_____
_____
_____
_____
_____
_____
_____
_____
_____
_____
_____
_____
_____
_____
_____

Are you angry about this situation? Express it here.

_____

_____

_____

_____

_____

_____

_____

_____

_____

_____

_____

_____

_____

_____

_____

_____

_____

_____

_____

_____

_____

_____

Are you angry about this situation? Express it here.

_____

_____

_____

_____

_____

_____

_____

_____

_____

_____

_____

_____

_____

_____

_____

_____

_____

_____

_____

_____

_____

_____

_____

Inhale

Exhale

Let it go...

Even if you can only do it

For a few moments at a time...

Anxiety Exercise

Write what is worrying you the most now

Describe the good outcome

Thinking rationally about outcomes can help relive your anxiety.

Anxiety Exercise

Describe the bad outcome you fear.

_____

_____

_____

_____

_____

_____

Describe the probable outcome

_____

_____

_____

_____

_____

_____

_____

Even though this is hard, you are strong enough to get through it.

Forgiveness

Do you need to forgive them? For what?

What might you need to ask forgiveness for from this person?

_____

_____

_____

_____

_____

_____

_____

_____

_____

_____

_____

_____

_____

_____

_____

_____

_____

_____

_____

_____

_____

_____

Being Mindful

Who else is hurting and how could I show them I care?

Grief can be a complex emotion. It can hit you when you least expect it. You will have days when you feel like you are happy and coping just fine. You will also have days when you are sad or weepy at the strangest or slightest things.

It's ok.

You need to honor your feelings. It's fine to employ avoidance tactics for a brief while, like watching too many shows or scrolling endlessly on your phone. But you do have to make the time and take the time to feel your emotions, explore them, honor them and then release them.

Just breathe. You're doing better than you think.

What self-care can you do to help the grief you're experiencing?
Write some things now and come back later and share what helped.

What self-care can you do to help the grief you're experiencing?
Write some things now and come back later and share what helped.

_____

_____

_____

_____

_____

_____

_____

_____

_____

_____

_____

_____

_____

_____

_____

_____

_____

_____

_____

_____

The
Grief Journal

Part Two:

Writing What You're Feeling

Daily, Weekly or Just

When You Feel Like It

Things to Remember:

Just let the feelings flow. Let your hands keep moving and don't stop to read what you've written.

Don't worry about spelling, grammar and punctuation.

Go ahead and lose control. Don't be logical—let your right brain have full reign.

Go ahead and dive into those messy, scary parts of the grief.

Most of all, be gentle and compassionate with yourself! This is big. No need to judge yourself here.

How are you feeling today?   Date:

How are you feeling today?   Date:_____

_____

_____

_____

_____

_____

_____

_____

_____

_____

_____

_____

_____

_____

_____

_____

_____

_____

_____

_____

_____

_____

_____

How are you feeling today?   Date:

How are you feeling today?　Date:

How are you feeling today?   Date:

How are you feeling today?   Date:

_____

_____

_____

_____

_____

_____

_____

_____

_____

_____

_____

_____

_____

_____

_____

_____

_____

_____

_____

_____

_____

_____

_____

How are you feeling today?   Date:

How are you feeling today?   Date:

How are you feeling today?   Date:

How are you feeling today?   Date:

How are you feeling today?   Date:

How are you feeling today? Date:_____

How are you feeling today?   Date:

How are you feeling today?   Date:

How are you feeling today?　Date:

How are you feeling today?   Date:_____

_____
_____
_____
_____
_____
_____
_____
_____
_____
_____
_____
_____
_____
_____
_____
_____
_____
_____
_____
_____
_____
_____
_____
_____
_____
_____

How are you feeling today?   Date:

How are you feeling today?   Date:

How are you feeling today?   Date:

How are you feeling today?   Date:

How are you feeling today?　Date:

How are you feeling today?   Date:

How are you feeling today?   Date:

How are you feeling today?   Date:

How are you feeling today?   Date:

How are you feeling today?　Date:_____

_____

_____

_____

_____

_____

_____

_____

_____

_____

_____

_____

_____

_____

_____

_____

_____

_____

_____

_____

_____

_____

_____

How are you feeling today?   Date:

How are you feeling today?   Date:

How are you feeling today?   Date:

How are you feeling today?   Date:

How are you feeling today?   Date:

How are you feeling today?   Date:

How are you feeling today?   Date:

How are you feeling today? Date:

How are you feeling today?   Date:_____

How are you feeling today?   Date:

How are you feeling today?   Date:

How are you feeling today?   Date:

How are you feeling today?   Date:

How are you feeling today?   Date:_____

How are you feeling today?　Date:

Memories

At this time, you are making memories, but not all of them are going to be good ones, especially if your loved one is suffering. It's very important to recall some good times and memories now and write them down, as they may be harder for your mind to access later when you are grieving your loved one's death.

This is something I wish I'd known, because I found it really hard for the first few weeks to remember much more than the final months of my sister's life and all that she endured. Do yourself a huge favor and write down some great memories on the pages that follow so you have them to look at later when your loved one is gone.

Dawn

Memories - Our Best Day(s) Together

_____
_____
_____
_____
_____
_____
_____
_____
_____
_____
_____
_____
_____
_____
_____
_____
_____
_____
_____
_____
_____
_____
_____

Memories - Our Best Day(s) Together

_____
_____
_____
_____
_____
_____
_____
_____
_____
_____
_____
_____
_____
_____
_____
_____
_____
_____
_____
_____
_____

Memories - Our Best Day(s) Together

_____
_____
_____
_____
_____
_____
_____
_____
_____
_____
_____
_____
_____
_____
_____
_____
_____
_____
_____
_____
_____
_____
_____
_____

Memories – Things We Loved to Do Together

Memories

Memories

Creativity

There are other ways you can explore your grief other than journaling. Sometimes art therapy is helpful. Use these blank pages to doodle . sketch or do some unstructured writing to let your feelings flow.

Creativity Page

Creativity Page

Creativity Page

Creativity Page

Creativity Page